Unit	Pupil Book	Pupil Book Focus	Pupil Book Practice	Pupil Book Extension	Resource Book Support	Resource Book Extension
15	**sentences**: subject and predicate*	dividing sentences into subject and predicate	identifying subjects and predicates/adding to subjects and predicates for interest	completing sentences with *I* or *me*	adding adjectives to subjects for interest/ adding adjectives and adverbs to predicates for interest	adding adjectives to given nouns and forming sentences with interesting predicates
16	**pronouns** repetition and clarity	listing nouns, pronouns and proper nouns in sentences	joining pairs of sentences and using pronouns/rewriting sentences for clarity	rewriting sentences – substituting pronouns for nouns to avoid repetition	joining pairs of sentences and using pronouns/ rewriting sentences to avoid repetition	constructing sentences from given sets of nouns and pronouns
17	**sentences**: relative clauses	identifying relative clauses and related nouns in sentences	completing sentences with *who* or *which*	adding relative clauses and main clauses / omitted relative pronoun	completing sentences with relative clauses/writing a description to include relative clauses	rewriting sentences with misplaced relative clauses
18	**verbs**: auxiliary*	identifying auxiliary verbs in sentences	completing sentences with *will* and *shall*; *have* and *has*; *was* and *were*	writing sentences with given verbs	choosing correct auxiliary verbs to complete sentences/changing auxiliary verbs to change the tense of sentences	adding auxiliary verbs to given verbs and using in sentences
19	**punctuation**: comma round-up*	explaining various uses of commas in sentences	adding missing commas to sentences	writing sentences with direct speech, frontal adverbial phrases and clauses from given stimuli	adding commas to sentences with direct speech, lists, frontal adverbials	writing conversation to include list, direct speech, split direct speech and frontal adverbials
20	**paragraphs**: adverbials	identifying adverbs, adverb phrases and adverb clauses in extended writing	descriptive writing using given adverbs and adverbial phrases	descriptive writing using own adverbials	identifying adverbials in descriptive writing/ continuing description	writing description from picture stimulus
21	**verbs**: prefixes	identifying prefix part of verbs	solving clues with prefix + verb	adding different prefixes to infinitive to form different verbs/using *co* + verb words in sentences	completing sentences with correct prefix + verb words/replacing phrases in sentences with one prefix + verb word/sentence writing	using unusual prefix + verb words in sentence writing
22	**confusing words***	correcting mistakes in sentences	correcting mistakes: *of – have*, *win – beat*, *it's – its*	sentence writing to show understanding	completing sentences with confusing words	sentence writing to show understanding: *accept – except*, *beside – besides*, *among – between* and *advice – advise*
23	**adverbs**: sequence words and phrases / possibility	completing sentences with given sequence adverbs	writing given groups of action in sentences with sequence adverbs and adverb phrases	categorising adverbs of possibility	identifying sequence adverbs in sentences/ rewriting sentences to avoid repeating *and then*/ sequencing actions done after school	converting recipe instructions into personal recount
24	**verbs**: auxiliary – modals	identifying modal verbs in sentences	completing sentences with *can* and *may*; *might* and *must*; *could*, *would* and *should*	writing sentences with given verbs	Identifying sentences that give permission or indicate ability to do something/ writing sentences with given verbs	writing sentences to show understanding of the various modal verbs
25	**sentences**: main, adverb and relative clauses	identifying main clauses in sentences	identifying adverb and relative clauses in sentences	adding relative clause to given main clauses/adding adverb clauses to given main clauses	extending given sentences in two ways with adverb and relative clauses	writing descriptive account to include adverb and relative clauses
26	**punctuation**: commas to avoid ambiguity	using commas to avoid ambiguity	adding commas to sentences to change meaning	explaining differences in meaning between pairs of sentences	adding commas to sentences to change meaning/adding commas so that adjective–noun + noun phrases become three nouns/writing silly sentences	explaining differences in meaning between pairs of sentences
27	**punctuation**: commas, brackets and dashes	identifying extra information in commas, brackets and dashes in sentences	adding punctuation for parenthesis in sentences	combining pairs of sentences by using parenthesis	identifying information in parenthesis in sentences/ adding given extra information to given sentences	combining pairs of sentences by using parenthesis/ incorporating given extra information into own sentences
28	**sentences**: improving writing	rewriting sentences to improve vocabulary	adding detail to simple sentences	using interesting vocabulary and adding detail to simple sentences	improving sentences with interesting vocabulary and detail	rewriting given passage to improve with vocabulary and detail

Singular and plural

Singular nouns are made plural in different ways.
You have learned:

	Singular	Plural
For most nouns, we add an s.	river	rivers
For nouns ending in s, ch, sh and x, we add es.	glass	glasses
	match	matches
	brush	brushes
	box	boxes
For nouns ending in a consonant + y, we take off the y and add ies.	baby	babies
For nouns ending with a vowel + y, we just add s.	valley	valleys
For nouns ending in o, we usually add es.	potato	potatoes
For musical nouns ending in o and for nouns ending in oo, we just add s.	piano	pianos
	cockatoo	cockatoos

Some nouns do not follow any of these rules.

They have a plural that is a different word.

singular	plural
child	children
goose	geese
person	people

Focus

A Make these singular nouns *plural*.

1 woman   **2** tooth   **3** ox

4 foot   **5** mouse   **6** postman

B Put each *plural noun* you have made in **A** in a sentence of your own.

Nelson Grammar

Pupil Book 5

OXFORD
UNIVERSITY PRESS

OXFORD
UNIVERSITY PRESS

Great Clarendon Street, Oxford, OX2 6DP, United Kingdom

Oxford University Press is a department of the University of Oxford.
It furthers the University's objective of excellence in research, scholarship,
and education by publishing worldwide. Oxford is a registered trade mark
of Oxford University Press in the UK and in certain other countries

Text © Wendy Wren 2014
Illustrations © A. Corazon Abierto and Kathryn Hudson 2014

The moral rights of the author have been asserted

First published 2014

British Library Cataloguing in Publication Data

Data available

ISBN: 978-1-4085-2392-6

9 10

Paper used in the production of this book is a natural, recyclable product made from
wood grown in sustainable forests. The manufacturing process conforms to the
environmental regulations of the country of origin.

Printed in China by Golden Cup

Acknowledgements

Series editor: John Jackman
Cover illustrations: Santiago Grasso
Page make-up: OKS Prepress, India

Contents

Book 5 Scope and Sequence

Unit	Pupil Book	Pupil Book Focus	Pupil Book Practice	Pupil Book Extension	Resource Book Support	Resource Book Extension
1	**singular and plural**: irregular plurals*	making singular nouns plural/writing sentences with plural nouns	completing sentences to show noun–verb agreement	singular and plural with same forms/nouns always plural	classifying nouns according to plural formation	forming plurals/sentence writing for noun–verb agreement
2	**pronouns and adjectives**: possessives*	identifying possessive pronouns and possessive adjectives in sentences	completing sentences with possessive pronouns and possessive adjectives	using possessive adjectives instead of possessive pronouns/using possessive pronouns instead of possessive adjectives	identifying possessive pronouns and possessive adjectives in sentences/writing sentences with possessive adjectives	rewriting sentences to use possessive adjectives instead of possessive pronouns/writing sentences with pairs of possessive pronouns/adjectives
3	**verbs**: round-up	forming verb tenses for given infinitives/identifying verb and tense in sentences	changing tenses in sentences	writing sentences with two actions	changing tenses in sentences	writing sentences about a given topic to include a given tense
4	**sentences**: direct speech*	identifying spoken words in sentences	completing and punctuating direct speech sentences	using speech bubbles to write a direct speech conversation and an indirect speech passage	punctuating various forms of direct speech sentences/completing and punctuating direct speech sentences/writing sentences with given phrases	rewriting and punctuating a narrative with direct speech
5	**adverbs**: clauses	identifying adverb clauses in sentences/linking adverb clause to verb	completing sentences with adverb clauses/rewriting sentences with frontal adverb clauses	joining sentences to make main clause + adverb clause	identifying adverb clauses/writing sentences with main clause + adverb clause and adverb clause + main clause	writing sentences with adverb clauses from given subordinating conjunctions
6	**nouns**: singular and plural possessive*	forming possessive nouns by adding apostrophes to singular and plural owners	rewriting given phrases using possessive nouns	correcting UK landmarks with apostrophes	identifying possessive nouns in sentences/forming singular and plural possessive phrases/sentence writing	correcting newspaper headlines with apostrophes
7	**sentences**: direct and indirect speech*	identifying direct and indirect speech and noting changes	converting direct speech sentences to indirect speech sentences/converting indirect speech sentences to direct speech sentences	writing conversation in direct speech/converting conversation to indirect speech	punctuating direct speech and indirect speech sentences/converting speech bubbles to direct speech and indirect speech sentences	writing direct and indirect speech sentences from picture stimuli
8	**sentences**: subject and predicate*	identifying sentence subjects and predicates	joining given subjects and predicates to make sensible sentences	completing sentences with interesting subjects and predicates	identifying subjects and predicates in sentences/adding interesting predicates to given subjects	writing pairs of sentences where a given noun is used as the subject and in the predicate
9	**homophones***	completing sentences with the correct homophone	choosing correct homophones to solve clues/using homophones in sentences	using unusual homophones in sentences to show understanding of meaning	choosing the correct homophone/writing sentences including pairs of homophones	homophone crossword
10	**verbs**: formed with *en*, *ate*, *ify* and *ise* suffixes	identifying verbs in sentences from noun and adjective root	forming verbs from nouns and adjectives to complete sentences	forming verbs from given adjectives/writing sentences	identifying verbs in sentences/forming verbs from given words to complete sentences/using given verbs in own sentences	forming verbs from more unusual nouns and adjectives/writing own sentences
11	**adjectives**: synonyms*	synonyms for given adjectives	rewriting sentences using more interesting adjectives	using unusual adjectives in sentence writing	classifying adjectives in synonym groups	writing synonym groups/using in sentence writing
12	**pronouns**: relative	completing sentences with relative pronouns	joining sentences with relative pronouns	completing sentences with *whose* and *whom*	joining sentences with relative pronouns/completing sentences	writing sentences using *who, which* and *that*
13	**homonyms***	identifying part of speech for homonyms	finding one word as the answer to two clues/sentence writing to show different meanings	identifying parts of speech within sentences/sentence writing to show different meanings	identifying parts of speech in sentences/solving clues/sentence writing to show different meanings	using pairs of homonyms as different parts of speech in sentences
14	**punctuation**: apostrophes*	identifying possession and contraction apostrophes in sentences	writing contractions and possessive nouns/adding missing apostrophes	identifying plurals, contractions and possessive nouns in sentences/adding missing apostrophes	identifying contractions and possessive nouns/writing contractions and possessive nouns	using given pairs of contractions and possessive nouns in sentences

4

* denotes content that is not specified in the National Curriculum for England (2014) but which will support children's wider knowledge and understanding of grammar.

A Copy the sentences into your book.

Write *is* or *are* to finish each sentence.

1 The mice _____ chewing through the rope.
2 The ox _____ working in the field.
3 The people _____ having a good time.

B Copy the sentences into your book.
Write *was* or *were* to finish each sentence.

1 The children _____ having tea.
2 The geese _____ swimming on the pond.
3 My tooth _____ hurting.

Extension

A Use a dictionary to find the *plural* of these nouns.

1 cod   2 mackerel   3 salmon
4 trout   5 sheep   6 deer

B Some words are always *plural*. Write labels for the pictures.

1 _____   2 _____

3 _____   4 _____

Pronouns and adjectives

Some pronouns show ownership or possession.

They are called possessive pronouns.

This dog is mine.

possessive pronoun

This car is ours.

These are all possessive pronouns:

mine	yours	his
hers	its	ours	theirs

Possessive adjectives tell us who possesses (owns) a noun.

This is my dog.

This is our car.

These are all possessive adjectives:

my	your	his	her	its	our	their

Focus

Read the pairs of sentences.

Find the *possessive pronoun* or *possessive adjective* in each sentence.

1 I think this jumper is hers.   This is her jumper.

2 Our house is painted white.   The white house is ours.

3 Is this their address?   This address is theirs.

4 That's my book.   That book is mine.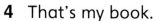

5 That lunchbox is hers.   She is eating her lunch.

A Copy the sentences into your book.

Replace the coloured words with a *possessive pronoun*.

1 My brother is older than <u>your brother</u> .

2 She has a blue bag. It must be <u>her bag</u> .

3 I think these are <u>our keys</u> .

B Copy and complete each sentence with a
possessive adjective.

1 The front tyre of the bicycle is flat but _____ back
tyre is OK.

2 "Put _____ coats in the cloakroom," the teacher said to
the class.

3 "I have forgotten _____ gloves and _____ hands are
cold," complained Sam.

Extension

A Rewrite each sentence using a *possessive
adjective* instead of a possessive pronoun.

> The first one has been done for you.

1 The boat is his.   This is his boat.

2 That dog is ours.

3 The black cat is mine.

4 That horse is theirs.

5 Is this football yours?

B Rewrite each sentence using a *possessive
pronoun* instead of a possessive adjective.

> The first one has been done for you.

1 It is my mistake.   The mistake is mine.

2 Are those her shoes?

3 These are our tickets.

4 That is their horse.

5 Is this your bicycle?

Verbs

This is a round-up of the verb tenses you know.

Verbs tell us what happens, has happened or will happen.

The tense of a verb tells us when something happens – in the past, the present or the future.

- past simple tense   He found a beautiful island.
- past progressive tense   He was travelling by boat.
- perfect tense   He has been around the world.
- past perfect tense   He had explored before.
- present simple tense   He likes exploring.
- present progressive tense   He is enjoying the trip.
- future tense   He will go to sea again.

Focus

A Say the verb *tenses* with *I* for each verb.

> past simple   past progressive   perfect   past perfect
> present simple   present progressive   future

1 to climb   **2** to eat   **3** to speak   **4** to draw   **5** to think   **6** to swim

B Identify the *verb* in each sentence and say which *tense* it is.

1   The cat was walking on the narrow wall.

2   The ladder fell with a crash.

3   He had forgotten his car keys.

4   We shall visit at the weekend.

5   I have seen that film before.

Practice

A Write these sentences in the *present progressive tense* and the *past progressive tense*.

1 I go for a walk.

2 They ride their horses.

3 We swim.

B Write these sentences in the *perfect tense* and the *past perfect tense*.

1 The birds flew away.

2 My strap broke.

3 They ate.

C Write these sentences in the *present simple tense* and the *past simple tense*.

1 I shall leave.

2 The sun will set.

3 You will go.

Extension

Write a sentence in the *past tense* and the *future tense* that includes each pair of actions.

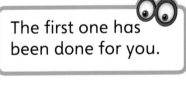
The first one has been done for you.

Action 1: happens first

Action 2: happens second

Action 1	**Action 2**
1 go to the park	go again tomorrow

I went to the park and I shall go again tomorrow.

2 finish loaf of bread	buy more
3 dig garden	plant seeds
4 wash clothes	iron clothes

Sentences

Direct speech is when we write the actual words that someone says.

- Speech marks go at the beginning and the end of the spoken words.
- Punctuation at the end of the spoken words goes before the speech marks.
- When a different person speaks, we begin a new line.

> "What time is it?" asked Jim.
>
> Tom looked at his phone and replied, "Three o'clock."

Sometimes we split the spoken words so we have to be very careful with the punctuation.

> "I would like to try mountain climbing," said Sue, "because I think it would be amazing!"

The sentence has been split by the words *said Sue*, so we use two sets of speech marks and put a comma after *said Sue*.

> "I'm thinking of trying mountain climbing," said Sue. "My friend says it is amazing!"

This time, Sue says two sentences. We still use two sets of speech marks, but we put a full stop after *said Sue* before we begin a new sentence.

Focus

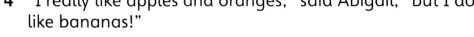

Say the *spoken words*.

1 "Finish your paintings," instructed the teacher, "and then tidy up."

2 "My cousin is coming at the weekend," said Amy, " and we are going to fly my kite."

3 "The car was parked outside the house," explained Mr Webb to the policeman. "It must have been stolen in the early hours of the morning."

4 "I really like apples and oranges," said Abigail, "but I don't like bananas!"

Copy each sentence and finish it with what you think the speaker might *say*.

Add the missing *punctuation*.

1 I've made an apple pie said Harry so _____

2 I took the dog to the vet said Rob because _____

3 When you have finished your homework said Mum can _____

4 I'm staying in said Dad until _____

5 I'll meet you at one o'clock said Joe outside _____

Read the speech bubbles.

A Write the conversation in *direct speech*.

B Write the conversation in *indirect speech*.

Adverbs

To make sentences more interesting we can use adverb clauses.

An adverb clause tells us more about the verb in the main clause.

An adverb clause:
- has a subject
- has a verb
- begins with a conjunction
- answers the questions Why, When or How.

Why?   The building caught fire because it was hit by lightning.
When? The building caught fire after lightning struck it twice.
How?   The building caught fire as if it was made of paper.

An adverb clause can come at the beginning of a sentence.
It is separated from the main clause by a comma.

Because it was hit by lightning, the building caught fire.
After the lightning struck twice, the building caught fire.
As if it was made of paper, the building caught fire.

Focus

- Say the *adverb clause* in every sentence.
- Say the *verb* each adverb clause tells us more about.

    1 The gardener dug a large hole before he planted the tree.

    2 Although she had followed the instructions carefully, the model didn't look right.

    3 I played on my computer game after I had learned my spellings.

    4 When you go into town, will you buy some apples?

    5 I will see the next patient when I have washed my hands.

    6 If we win today, we are in the final!

A Copy the sentences.

Complete the *adverb clauses*.

1 The audience laughed when _____.

2 I have bought new pencils because _____.

3 The photographer set up his camera before _____.

4 We enjoyed the film even though _____.

5 The team played well although _____.

B Rewrite your sentences, putting the *adverb clause* at the beginning.

Extension

The first one has been done for you.

Join each pair of sentences, making the second sentence an *adverbial clause*.

1 I took my umbrella.   It was going to rain.

I took my umbrella because it was going to rain.

2 He liked wearing his trainers.   They hurt his feet.

3 I did the crossword.   I read the newspaper.

4 The people screamed.   The lightning struck.

5 I went to bed.   My friends had gone.

Nouns

A possessive noun tells us who owns something.

When there is only one owner, we add apostrophe s ('s) to the owner.

the wolf's howl

the child's doll

When there is more than one owner:

- if the owners already end in s, just add an apostrophe
- if the owners do not end in s, add apostrophe s

the wolves' howls

the children's dolls

Write these in your book.

Add *apostrophes* to the owners.

Be careful! The owners are singular and plural.

1 the leafs stalk
2 the leaves stalks
3 the oxs tail
4 the oxens tails
5 the ladys house
6 the ladies houses
7 the volcanos eruptions
8 the volcanoes eruptions
9 the countrys flag
10 the countries flags

Practice

A Change the phrases below by using *possessive nouns*.

All the owners are plural.

1 the journey of the elephants
2 the handles of the brushes
3 the block of the knives
4 the fillings of the teeth
5 the tails of the foxes

B Use these *possessive nouns* in sentences of your own.

1 the people's   2 my rabbits'   3 Africa's
4 Sam's   5 the policemen's   6 the pupils'

Extension

These are places you can visit in the UK.

The *apostrophes* are missing.

Copy the names and add the missing *apostrophes*.

1

Cleopatras Needle (London)

2

Fingals Cave (Inner Hebrides)

3

Poets Corner (London)

4

St Catherines Point Lighthouse (Isle of Wight)

5

The Giants Causeway (Ireland)

6
St Pauls Cathedral (London)

17

Direct speech is when we write the actual words that someone says.

- **Speech marks** go at the beginning and the end of the spoken words.
- **Punctuation** at the end of the spoken words goes before the speech marks.
- When a different person speaks, we begin a new line.

> "Could you tell me the way to the railway station?" the lady asked.
> "I'm sorry," Gina replied, "but I don't know. If you ask in the shop, I'm sure Mr Fold will know."
> "Thank you very much. I'll do that," replied the lady.

Indirect speech is when we write about what someone has said.
- We don't use the actual spoken words.
- we don't use speech marks.

> A lady asked Gina if she could tell her the way to the railway station. Gina said that she didn't know. She suggested the lady go into the shop and ask Mr Fold. She was sure he would know. The lady thanked Gina and said she would ask in the shop.

Indirect speech is also called reported speech.

Focus

Read each pair of sentences. Discuss:
- which is *direct speech* and which is *indirect speech*
- what words have changed.

1 "Today, we will look at speech in stories," said Mrs Gold.
    Mrs Gold said that today they would look at speech in stories.
2 "You have to think carefully about what your characters say," she told us.
    She told us that we had to think carefully about what our characters say.
3 "A reader can learn a lot about a character by what they say," said Mrs Gold.
    Mrs Gold said that a reader could learn a lot about a character by what they say.

A Write each of these sentences using *indirect speech*.

1 "We need an ambulance!" screamed the driver.
2 The Mayor said, "I would like to welcome you all to our city."

3 "If you wait just a minute," explained the librarian, "I will show you where to find the biography section."
4 "Rain like this is a disaster," groaned the farmer. "It will ruin the crops!"

B Write each of these sentences using *direct speech*.

1 Paul wanted to know if anyone was thirsty.
2 Sue said that she was good at map reading.
3 My friend invited me to her birthday party.
4 The team was told by the manager that they had to do better in the second half.

Extension

A Write a conversation in *direct speech* between a shopkeeper and a customer.

The shopkeeper is polite. The customer is rather rude.

Remember to:
• use *speech marks* and other *punctuation*
• begin a *new line* when a different person speaks
• use synonyms for *said*.

B Write the same conversation in *indirect speech*.

Remember that you do *not* need speech marks because you are not writing the actual words that were spoken.

Sentences

A sentence has two parts.

The subject is the person or thing that the sentence is about.

The predicate is the rest of the sentence.

Subject	Predicate
The eagle	is a large bird.
My bucket	has a hole in it.
Rabbits	live in burrows.
I	would like a kitten.

To find the subject of a sentence, first find the verb.

My bucket has a hole in it.   verb = has

Ask who or what has in the sentence.   my bucket (has a hole)

The subject is my bucket.

Focus

A What is the *subject* in each sentence?

1 I have hurt my knee.

2 Sharks live in the sea.

3 The Queen lives in a palace.

4 The horses are in the stables.

5 Roger is travelling to India.

B What is the *predicate* in each sentence?

1 The bakery opens at nine o'clock.

2 We decided to go to the park.

3 The river bursts its banks.

4 Our garage is big enough for two cars.

5 My friends and I like to play football.

Join each *subject* with the correct *predicate* to make a sentence.

Subject	Predicate
1 The cottage	watched the match.
2 I	was very exciting.
3 The race	was near the stream.
4 A large crowd	wrote the answers carefully.
5 Sam	am paddling a canoe.

Extension

A Write an interesting *subject* for each *predicate*.

1 _____ fell into the pond.

2 _____ were afraid of the dark.

3 _____ frightened my brother.

4 _____ left her bag on the bus.

5 _____ flapped its huge wings.

B Write an interesting *predicate* for each of these subjects.

1 The rotting apple _____.

2 The huge forest _____.

3 They _____.

4 Some birds _____.

5 This interesting old coin _____.

Homophones

Homophones are words that sound the same BUT

- are spelled differently
- have a different meaning.

Using the wrong homophone can make what we write ridiculous!

She put the flour in the vase.
What the writer means is:
She put the flower in the vase.

He cooked a stake for his dinner.
What the writer means is:
He cooked a steak for his dinner.

The chef added time to the stew.
What the writer means is:
The chef added thyme to the stew.

Focus

Choose the correct *homophone* from the brackets to complete each sentence.

1 The train leaves in one _____.   our/hour

2 I will _____ you by the station clock.   meat/meet

3 Can you _____ the tickets?   buy/by

4 Make sure you get the _____ ones.   write/right

5 I _____ which tickets to get!   know/no

6 Sorry! I'm just _____ excited.   sew/so

7 I can _____ how excited you are!   hear/here

8 _____ you there!   sea/see

A Solve the clues with the correct *homophone*.

1	A cat has four of these.	paws/pause
2	You can find one of these around a castle.	mote/moat
3	You build sandcastles on this.	beech/beach
4	This is a kind of corn.	maize/maze
5	Some houses have a flight of these.	stares/stairs

B Use the different *homophones* in sentences of your own.

Extension

These pairs of *homophones* are more unusual.

Use each of them in a sentence of your own to show you clearly understand the meaning.

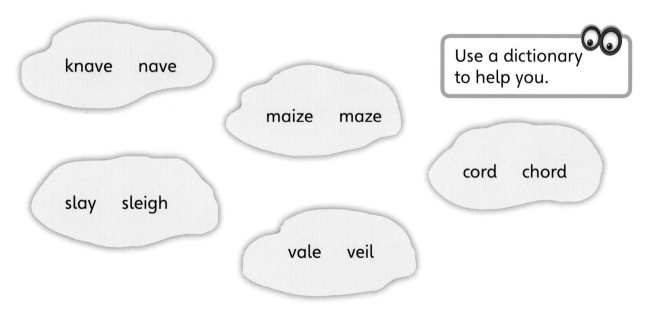

knave   nave

maize   maze

Use a dictionary to help you.

cord   chord

slay   sleigh

vale   veil

Verbs

 These words are all in the same word family.

Some verbs are formed from nouns and adjectives by adding the suffixes:

ate   en   ify   ise

noun	+ ate = verb
medicine	medicate
captive	captivate

abstract noun	+ en = verb	adjective	+ en = verb
fright	frighten	sharp	sharpen
strength	strengthen	flat	flatten

abstract noun	ify = verb	adjective	+ ify = verb
horror	horrify	pure	purify
beauty	beautify	simple	simplify

noun	+ ise = verb	adjective	+ ify = verb
computer	computerise	equal	equalise
pedestrian	pedestrianise	fertile	fertilise

Focus

Find the *verb* in each sentence.

Say whether it is formed from a *noun* or an *adjective*.

1 The moon brightened the cloudy sky.

2 We shall fertilise the crops.

3 Europeans colonised America.

4 Parents were notified about the school closure.

5 The cement will harden in a few hours.

A Copy the sentences.

Use the *nouns* in the box to make *verbs* to complete the sentences.

apology   vandal   drama   light   terror

1 Someone has _____ the bus shelter.

2 If I take one of those bags, it will _____ the load.

3 The boy _____ for kicking his ball into the flowers.

4 The bandits _____ the townspeople.

5 We will read the short story and then _____ it.

B Use the *adjectives* in the box to make *verbs* to complete the sentences.

domestic   hypnotic   mobile   tight   wide

1 The army commander had to _____ his troops.

2 The magician _____ a member of the audience.

3 They will have to _____ the road when the new houses are built.

4 _____ the rope before the horse escapes!

5 Wild animals were _____ by prehistoric people.

Make a *verb* from each adjective.

Use each *verb* in a sentence of your own.

1 straight   **2** deep

3 sad   **4** bright

5 glamorous   **6** legal

Adjectives

We always need to read through what we write to see if we can improve it.

Often, we use very boring adjectives.

> I got a nice present for my birthday.
>
> We saw a big elephant at the zoo.
>
> The flowers were pretty.

We can improve these sentences by using more interesting adjectives.

> I got a wonderful present for my birthday.
>
> We saw an enormous elephant at the zoo.
>
> The flowers were magnificent.

Synonyms are words that mean the same or nearly the same.

nice	and	wonderful	=	synonyms
big	and	enormous	=	synonyms
pretty	and	magnificent	=	synonyms

Focus

Can you think of interesting *synonyms* for these *adjectives*?

1

cross

2

bad

3

boring

4

broken

5

quiet

6

happy

7

cold

8

dirty

9

easy

10

exciting

11

kind

12

heavy

A Rewrite these sentences using a more interesting *adjective* for *nice*.

   1 We had a nice meal.

   2 I had a nice chat with my friend.

   3 I like nice shoes.

   4 She looked very nice in her new clothes.

   5 He scored a nice goal.

   6 We had a nice time.

B Rewrite these sentences using a more interesting *adjective* for *little*.

   1 The little mouse scurried across the floor.

   2 You have little feet!

   3 He collects little toy soldiers.

   4 You can't see germs with your eyes because they are little.

Extension

These are unusual *adjectives*.
Use them in sentences of your own.

1 solitary   **2** enchanting

3 fashionable   **4** exquisite

5 pallid   **6** immaculate

> If you are not sure what the adjectives mean, use a dictionary.

UNIT 12 Pronouns

A pronoun takes the place of a noun.

> The driver parked the delivery van outside the shop.

> He parked the delivery van outside the shop.

The following pronouns are called relative pronouns.

who	whom	whose	which	that

Relative pronouns are special because they do two jobs.

1 They take the place of nouns.

2 They act as conjunctions, and they are related to the noun that comes before them in a sentence.

> Conjunctions are joining words.

> I have a sister.
> My sister is younger than me.
> I have a sister who is younger than me.

> The passenger caught the train.
> The train was going to Cardiff.
> The passenger caught the train which was going to Cardiff.

Who is used for people.

Which/That are used for animals and things.

 Focus

Copy the sentences.

Use the relative pronoun *who* or *which* to complete each one.

1 That's the badger _____ comes into our garden.

2 This letter is from my penfriend _____ lives in America.

3 I want to go to the park _____ has a boating lake.

4 The doctor _____ visited me was very kind.

5 The topic, _____ we are doing at school, is very interesting.

Copy and join each pair of sentences using *who*, *which* or *that*.

1 I found an old coin. The coin was used in Roman times.
2 We have two cousins. Our cousins live by the sea.
3 Sam bought a book. The book was about fishing.
4 He waved to his friend. His friend was on the other side of the road.
5 Sally is a nurse. Sally works with old people.

Extension

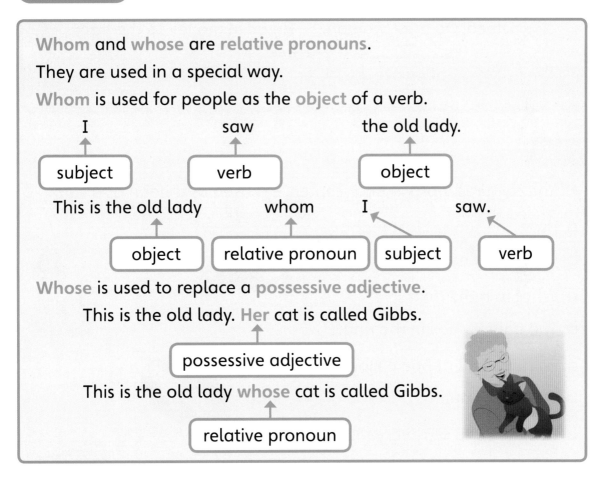

Whom and **whose** are **relative pronouns**.
They are used in a special way.
Whom is used for people as the **object** of a verb.

I   saw   the old lady.

| subject | verb | object |

This is the old lady   whom   I   saw.

| object | relative pronoun | subject | verb |

Whose is used to replace a **possessive adjective**.
This is the old lady. **Her** cat is called Gibbs.

| possessive adjective |

This is the old lady **whose** cat is called Gibbs.

| relative pronoun |

Copy and complete each sentence with *whom* or *whose*.

1 I know the man _____ car was stolen.
2 From _____ did you borrow this book?
3 _____ bag is this?
4 This is Fred _____ brother went to school with me.

Homonyms are words that are different parts of speech, BUT they:

• sound the same
• are spelled the same.

They sail at the weekend.

> verb

They took the sail down.

> noun

He helped the poor woman.

> adjective

He gave money to the poor.

> noun

Focus

Say if the *coloured* word in each sentence is used as a *noun* or a *verb*.

1 a I saw the sun set last night.

   b We need a new set of glasses.

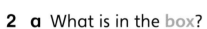

2 a What is in the box?

   b The fighters box in the ring.

3 a Ring the bell at one o'clock.

   b That's a beautiful ring you are wearing.

4 a I enjoyed the play very much.

   b Do you play a musical instrument?

5 a That fence post is rotten!

   b Post the letter before midday.

A The answer to each pair of clues is a *homonym*.
Write the *homonym*.

1 **a** small rodent   **b** part of a computer

2 **a** part of the body   **b** a large box with a lock

3 **a** jump over a rope   **b** leave out

4 **a** an amount of money   **b** to hit hard

5 **a** only one   **b** the bottom of your foot

B Choose your *homonym* for two of the clues in **A**.

Write two sentences for each *homonym* showing you understand the different meanings.

Extension

A Which part of speech is each *homonym* in bold?

1 **a** He fought hard and was victorious.

   b There was a hard frost on the ground in the morning.

2 **a** I was trying to mend the watch and a spring fell out.

   b There are some antelopes that spring as they run.

3 **a** You can't park the car here!

   b Play in the park where it is safe.

B Write sentences to show two meanings for each of these words.

1 rest

2 grave

3 race

4 bank

There are two uses of the apostrophe:
1   the apostrophe of contraction
    If something contracts it gets smaller.

    Contractions are words that are smaller.
    • A letter is (or letters are) missed out.
    • An apostrophe goes in place of the missing letter or letters.

    We are diving.   We're diving.
    You are diving.   You're diving.

    He has finished the book.   He's finished the book.
    I have finished the book.   I've finished the book.

    I do not like cheese.   I don't like cheese.
    She is not happy.   She isn't happy.

2   the apostrophe of possession
    This apostrophe shows us who owns what.
    It makes possessive nouns.

    the shoes belonging to the clown   = the clown's shoes
    the hats belonging to the girls   = the girls' hats
    the toys belonging to the children = the children's toys

Focus

Find the word with the *apostrophe* in each sentence.

Say whether the apostrophe is for *contraction* or *possession*.

1   Many people don't like football.

2   The puppies' basket was warm and snug.

3   I'm not sure how to do this sum!

4   Why can't you help me?

5   Everyone's coats were soaked.

6   The geese's webbed feet slapped on the ground.

A Write the *contractions*.

   1 do not   **2** would not   **3** you are   **4** it is

   5 they have **6** is not   **7** let us   **8** I am

B Write the *possessive nouns*.

   1 the dog belonging to the boy   **2** the lorries belonging to the men

   3 the scarves belonging to the ladies   **4** the pot belonging to the chimney

   5 the cave belonging to the bears   **6** the skin belonging to the tomato

C Copy the words and add the missing *apostrophes*.

   1 wont   **2** cant   **3** hes   **4** youve

   5 were   **6** Ive   **7** wouldnt **8** theyre

D Copy the words and add the missing *apostrophes*.

   1 the horses hoof   **2** the ships captain

   3 the magicians trick **4** the elephants trunks

   5 my aunts flowers   **6** the babies mothers

Read each sentence carefully.

Decide if the words ending in *s* are:

   • *plurals*   • *contractions*   • *possessive nouns*.

Copy the sentences and add the apostrophes.

1 The schools football team won all the matches this term.

2 Nobodys going anywhere until your desks are tidy.

3 Many peoples idea of a good time is visiting theme parks.

4 The explorers journeys took him to many countries.

5 Its great to see that the birds nests are safe.

Sentences

Sentences have two parts.

The subject is the person or thing written about.

The predicate is the rest of the sentence.

[subject]

(The cottage)(was in the wood.)

[predicate]

This is a very simple sentence that does not tell us very much. It is not very interesting!

We can make the sentence more interesting by adding to the subject.

[subject]

(The old, tumbledown cottage)(was in the wood.)

[predicate]

We can make the sentence even more interesting by adding to the predicate.

[subject]

(The old, tumbledown cottage)(was in the dark, gloomy wood.)

[predicate]

Split each sentence into two parts: (a) the subject, and (b) the predicate.

1 The pillow was on the bed.

2 I like to go to the pictures.

3 The priest wore a cloak.

4 This battery is flat.

5 Rob is cooking fish.

A Copy each sentence. Underline the *subject*.

1 The butterfly sat on a leaf.
2 Monkeys live in the jungle.
3 A package was delivered.

B Write each sentence from **A**, making the *subject* more interesting.

C Copy each sentence. Underline the *predicate*.

1 The flag was hoisted up the pole.
2 I went to the shops.
3 Ali has a bicycle.

D Write each sentence from **B**, making the *predicate* more interesting.

Extension

> **I** is used as the **subject** of a sentence.
>
> subject
>
> I am doing my homework.
>
> **Me** is used in the **predicate** of a sentence.
>
> Mum is taking **me** to the match.
>
> predicate

Copy and complete each sentence with *I* or *me*.

1 _____ saw a spider in the old, dark house.

2 Will you get _____ a drink?

3 Katy and _____ are going swimming.

4 The dog frightened Becky and _____.

Using pronouns in sentences helps to avoid repetition.

James took James' bicycle and James went to the shop.

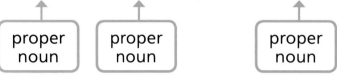

proper noun	proper noun		proper noun

James took his bicycle and he went to the shop.

proper noun	pronoun	pronoun

Sometimes, using pronouns makes a sentence unclear.

James took it to the shop.

What is it?

his bicycle?   his dog?   his basket ball?

Focus

List the *nouns*, *proper nouns* and *pronouns* in each sentence.

1 I asked my friend to give me her new phone number.

2 Mr Jones was a shopkeeper and he was very friendly.

3 The ferry crossed the Channel from Dover to Calais.

4 The sunset was so beautiful that I took a photograph of it.

5 Although I was very tired, I wanted to stay up to see the meteor shower.

A Copy and join each pair of sentences with a *conjunction*.

Replace *nouns* with *pronouns* to avoid repetition.

1 The robbers broke into the house.   The robbers stole the jewels.

2 I took my cat to the vet.   My cat had been in a fight.

3 Alice caught the ball.   Alice scored a goal.

4 We washed the baby's hands.   The baby had her milk.

5 The leaves fell off the trees.   The trees were bare.

B Copy the sentences into your book.

Replace any *pronoun* with a *noun* where necessary to make the meaning clear.

1 Give it to them.

2 Can you wrap it up for me?

3 He needs it to give it to him.

4 Find it and take it to her.

5 It took it and ran away with it in its mouth.

> Think carefully. You do not have to replace every pronoun.

Extension

Rewrite these sentences. Use *pronouns* instead of *nouns* to avoid repetition.

1 Bill went fishing so that Bill could catch a fish for Bill's tea.

2 The girl went into the shop because the girl wanted to buy the girl a new pen.

3 The scouts pitched the scouts' tents so the scouts would be near the river.

4 Sally and I got up early so Sally and I could visit Sally's aunt.

5 The tortoise raced the hare and the tortoise won because the hare went to sleep.

To make sentences more interesting, we can use relative clauses.

A relative clause:
- begins with a relative pronoun or with

| who | whose | which | that |

| where | when |

Another name for a relative clause is an adjective clause.

- tells us more about a noun or pronoun in the main clause.

main clause = We went to the shop

relative clause = that sold camping equipment.

We went to the shop that sold camping equipment.

main clause = The nurse took care of the man

relative clause = who had broken his arm

The nurse took care of the man who had broken his arm.

We use who when we are writing about a person.

I thanked the girl who had found my bag.

We use which/that when we are writing about an animal or thing.

Can you find the key which fits this lock?

I saw the birds that are nesting in our garage.

Focus

Copy the sentences.

Underline the *relative clause* in each sentence.

Put a ring around the *noun* it tells us about.

1 I delivered the package which my mother had given me.
2 Mark wrote to his friend who lives in Brazil.
3 This is the badge that I bought at the zoo.
4 Here is the shop where I bought my bicycle.
5 The lady thanked the young girl who had helped her across the road.

Copy and complete the sentences with *who* or *which*.

1 They travelled by a bus _____ took a long time.

2 I have thrown away the chair _____ had a broken arm.

3 Will you find someone _____ can take care of this dog?

4 There were several passengers _____ had lost their tickets.

5 Find the pencil _____ has a rubber on the end.

Extension

> You can leave out the relative pronoun **that** from some sentences.
> The cake that I baked was tasty.
> The cake I baked was tasty.

A Copy and complete each sentence by adding a *relative clause* to the main clause to make interesting sentences.

1 He baked the bread _____

2 The police went to the house _____

3 They looked for the girl _____

4 We visited our uncle _____

B Copy and complete each sentence by adding a *main clause* to the relative clause to make interesting sentences.

1 _____ who likes to play football.

2 _____ which grows in our garden.

3 _____ that I like best.

4 _____ which fell on our house.

Verbs

Sometimes verbs are made up of more than one word.

The verbs to be and to have are often used with other verbs to make different tenses.

We call these verbs auxiliary verbs.

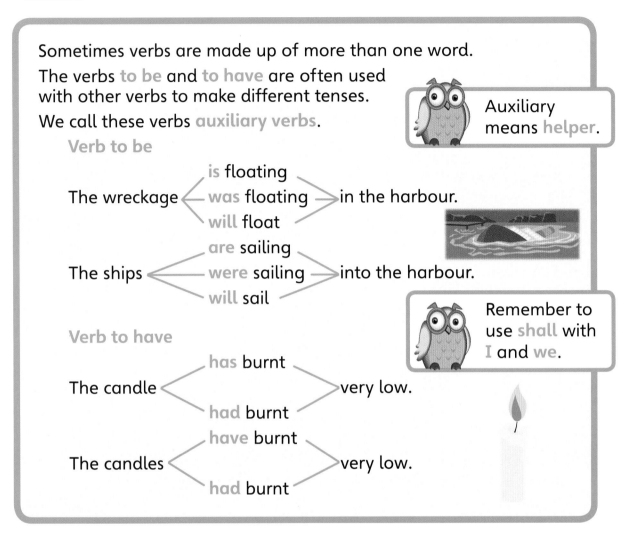

Auxiliary means helper.

Verb to be

The wreckage
- is floating
- was floating
- will float

in the harbour.

The ships
- are sailing
- were sailing
- will sail

into the harbour.

Remember to use shall with I and we.

Verb to have

The candle
- has burnt
- had burnt

very low.

The candles
- have burnt
- had burnt

very low.

Focus

What is the *auxiliary verb* in each sentence?

1 The picture was hanging on the wall.

2 I have forgotten to do my homework!

3 The horse is galloping across the fields.

4 The shield will keep you safe.

5 I am making a cake for my brother's birthday.

6 The explorers were trekking through the mountains.

7 He has bought a new computer game.

8 We shall miss the bus!

A Copy and complete the sentences with the auxiliary verbs *will* and *shall*.

1 I _____ write very neatly in my new exercise book.

2 You _____ need gloves because it is very cold.

3 He _____ find these sums difficult.

4 We _____ pack our suitcases in the morning.

B Copy and complete the sentences with the auxiliary verbs *have* and *has*.

1 They _____ won the relay race.

2 She _____ painted a beautiful picture.

3 I _____ lost my dinner money!

4 Ben and Tim _____ built a snowman.

C Copy and complete the sentences with the auxiliary verbs *was* and *were*.

1 The car _____ stuck in the mud.

2 It _____ snowing in the night.

3 They _____ collecting eggs from the hens.

4 Kim and I _____ going to a friend's house after school.

Extension

Write sentences using these pairs of verbs.

Underline the *auxiliary verb* in each sentence.

1 has received	**2** will recognise
3 have finished	**4** shall try
5 is dodging	**6** was carrying
7 am cooking	**8** were talking
9 had finished	**10** are planning

Punctuation

Commas are very important. We use them in several ways.

When we write a list in a sentence we use commas.

We join the last two things in the list with and, but or or.

> She picked up her hat, backpack and keys.

When we write direct speech, we use commas.

> "There's an orange glow in the sky," said the ranger.

> "There's an orange glow in the sky," said the ranger, "and I think it's a forest fire!"

When we put an adverb phrase or clause before the main clause, we use commas to separate them.

> After she saw the fire, she rang for help.

Focus

Say why *commas* are used in each sentence.

1 Would you like tea, coffee, milk or juice?

2 "This is a very difficult game," said the boy.

3 Later that day, the rain fell in torrents.

4 Although I like fruit, I'm not keen on apples.

5 His clothes were dirty, his feet sore, his head ached and his hands were bruised.

6 "Put the table in the kitchen," instructed the lady, "and that box upstairs."

Copy the sentences. Add the missing *commas*.

1 "Will you go up into the loft" asked Mum "and bring down the cases?"
2 The box contained old books a board game a broken mobile phone and some comics.
3 Because I am very tired I won't be staying late.
4 Early in the morning the birds began their dawn chorus.
5 We saw sheep grazing cows being milked horses galloping and chickens scratching in the dirt.

Extension

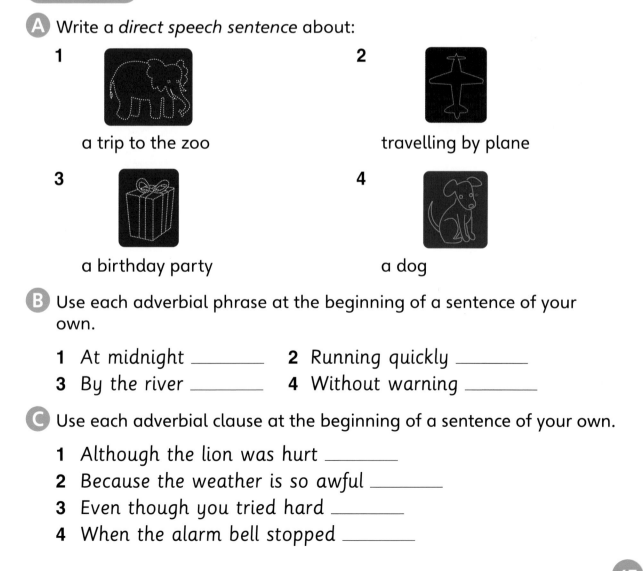

A Write a *direct speech sentence* about:

1
    a trip to the zoo

2
    travelling by plane

3
    a birthday party

4
    a dog

B Use each adverbial phrase at the beginning of a sentence of your own.

    1 At midnight _____
    2 Running quickly _____
    3 By the river _____
    4 Without warning _____

C Use each adverbial clause at the beginning of a sentence of your own.

    1 Although the lion was hurt _____
    2 Because the weather is so awful _____
    3 Even though you tried hard _____
    4 When the alarm bell stopped _____

Paragraphs

A paragraph is a group of sentences about one main idea.

Having paragraphs in descriptions makes it easier for the reader to follow.

We often start a new paragraph in a description when the place changes.

Paragraph 1 → We moved into our new house last week. The first thing I did was to rush upstairs to my new room and look out of the window.

Paragraph 2 → Beneath the window was a long, overgrown garden. Weeds had taken over everywhere. Piled near the wall, I could see bits of rusting bikes and an old mattress.

Paragraph 3 → Beyond the garden, there was a river winding its way across flat, green fields. It glittered in the sunlight and birds wheeled and soared above it.

Paragraph 4 → To the right, there was a small group of trees and to the left, a deserted cottage with broken windows and a leaky roof.

Paragraph 5 → In the distance, the huge, grey bulk of the power station looked dark and menacing against the skyline.

Focus

Read the description.

What *adverbs*, *adverb phrases* and *adverb clauses* tell you where:

1 the writer rushed to?

2 the garden is?

3 the bits of rusting bikes are?

4 the river is?

5 the birds are?

6 the small group of trees is?

7 the deserted cottage is?

8 the power station is?

Write a *description* about what you can see out of your window.

The beginning of each *paragraph* is going to let the reader know the *position* of what you are describing.

Here are some useful *adverbs*.

> above   behind   below   north   south
> east   west   outside   towards   nearby

Here are some useful *adverb phrases*.

> just beyond   over the road   next to   in the distance
> far away   right below   over there   in front of

Write your description and underline the *adverbs* and *adverbial phrases* you use.

Extension

Using *adverbs*, *adverb phrases* and *adverb clauses*, write a description of an alien planet in three paragraphs.

Paragraph 1:   You climb down from your spaceship.
              What can you see?

Paragraph 2:   You walk some distance from your spaceship.
              What can you see?

Paragraph 3:   You get to the edge of a huge crater and look down.
              What can you see?

Letters added to the front of a word are called a prefix.

happy   unhappy   legal   illegal

Prefixes can be added to verbs to change their meaning.

prefix	= dis	meaning	= not / opposite
agree	disagree	trust	distrust

prefix	= mis	meaning	= wrongly / badly
behave	misbehave	treat	mistreat

prefix	= over	meaning	= too much
work	overwork	load	overload

prefix	= re	meaning	= again / back
do	redo	charge =	recharge

prefix	= co	meaning	= together
exist	coexist	star	co-star

prefix	= out	meaning	= more / better
number	outnumber	do	outdo

prefix	= under	meaning	= not enough
cook	undercook	value	undervalue

Focus

Copy the verbs. Underline the *prefix*.

Use a dictionary for words you don't know.

1 disbelieve   2 misjudged   3 overcome

4 restart   5 co-write   6 outlive

7 undercharge   8 dislike   9 misplace

10 overrate   11 reunite   12 outstrip

Choose the correct *prefix* from the box to solve the clues.

out	mis	re	under	dis	over

1 If you do not do as you are told, you   _____ obey

2 If you give the main ideas of a plan, you   _____ line

3 If you ask too little money for something, you   _____ charge

4 If you drive faster than another car, you   _____ take

5 If you give someone incorrect information, you   _____ inform

6 If you begin again, you   _____ start

Extension

Adding a **different prefix** to the same **verb** changes the meaning.

to charge

recharge	**under**charge	**over**charge
to charge again	to charge too little	to charge too much

Ⓐ Each of these verbs can take two *prefixes*.

Write each new verb.

Use each new verb in a sentence of your own.

1 to appear   2 to place   3 to rate

4 to pay   5 to cover   6 to do

Ⓑ What do these 'co' verbs mean?

Use each in a sentence of your own.

1 cooperate   2 co-author   3 co-host

4 co-pilot   5 coordinate   6 coexist

Confusing words

Some words are very confusing.

- **it's** and **its**

  it's = it is

  It's my birthday.

  its = belonging to

  Its paw is hurt.

- **win** and **beat**

  win = to come first/get a prize

  I won the race.

  I won the trophy.

  beat = to be better than

  I beat my opponent.

  I beat everyone.

- **of** and **have**

  of = preposition

  The bouquet of flowers was beautiful.

  have = verb

  I have a beautiful bouquet of flowers.

- **practice and practise**

  practice = noun

  It is good practice to play every day.

  practise = verb

  I practise the piano every day.

Focus

Discuss and correct the *mistake* in each sentence.

1 I could of cried when I heard what happened.

2 I won you in that match.

3 The house had a leaky roof and it's windows were broken.

4 If I practice, I will get better.

5 I came first and beat the prize.

6 The netball practise went well.

7 Its difficult to know what to do.

A Sometimes, the writer has confused *of* and *have*.

Copy and correct the sentences.

1 I of heard of your accident.
2 Of course, I should of said something.
3 If I had been at school, I could of helped you but I of been ill.

B Sometimes, the writer has confused *win* and *beat*.

Copy and correct the sentences.

1 If I beat the race, I win the cup.
2 I can win you any day.
3 He won his friend by five metres.

C Sometimes, the writer has confused *it's* and *its*.

Copy and correct the sentences.

1 Its no good, it's tyre is flat!
2 Its a long walk to the garage.
3 Its probably shut at this time of night!

Extension

Write a sentence that contains each pair of words.

The first one has been done for you.

1 lend   borrow

If you lend me your pen, you can borrow my rubber.

2 teach   learn

3 where   were

4 practice   practise

5 their   they're

Adverbs

These are called sequence adverbs.

Adverbs that tell us when things are done are useful if we are writing an explanation, or recounting something that we did.

Very young children often just use and then.

> I woke up early and then I got out of bed. I went to get washed. I cleaned my teeth and then I brushed my hair. I went downstairs and then I had my breakfast and then I packed my bag for school.

There are much better words and phrases to show the sequence of actions.

> I woke up early and got out of bed. Next, I began to get ready for school. First of all, I went to the bathroom. After I had washed, I cleaned my teeth and lastly brushed my hair. Finally, I went downstairs for breakfast. Afterwards, I packed my bag for school.

Using these sorts of words and phrases rather than and then makes our writing much more interesting and cohesive.

Focus

Copy and complete the sentences with *sequence adverbs* from the box.

next	before	firstly	finally	after

1 _____ we had finished supper, we washed up.

2 You must wash your hands _____ you touch food.

3 I put the washing in the machine. _____ I put in the powder.

4 After many tries, she _____ got the lid off the jar!

5 _____, I have to say that I am surprised at you.

Write a sentence for each of the three actions in each group.

Use *sequence adverbs* (words or phrases) to show the order in which they happened.

Try to use different sequence adverbs in each group. The first one has been done for you.

Group 1

- found an injured bird
- put it in a box
- took it to the vet

Last night, we found an injured bird. *At first*, we put it in a box to keep warm. *Eventually*, we took it to the vet.

Group 2

- paddled in the sea
- built sandcastles
- had a picnic

Group 3

- picked blackberries
- made pie
- ate the pie

Group 4

- tackled a player
- passed the ball
- scored a goal

Extension

You can use adverbs to say how possible or likely something is.
Perhaps we will go to the park today.
We will definitely go to the park today.

Here are some more adverbs showing possibility.

certainly definitely probably possibly maybe surely perhaps

Copy the adverbs and sort them under the headings below.

Very possible   **Quite possible**   **Might be possible**

UNIT 24 Verbs

Sometimes **verbs** are made up of more than one word.

These verbs are made up of **auxiliary** or **helper** verbs + main verb.

This group of **auxiliary verbs** is very useful.

may	might	could
can	must	would
		should

These are called **modal** verbs.

Can and **may**:

He **can** answer that question.

He **may** leave the room.

Might and **must**:

You **must** clean the floor.

I **might** catch an early train.

Could, would and **should**:

I **could** meet you at twelve o'clock.

They **would** enjoy a picnic today.

You **should** wear a helmet when you ride your bike.

Focus

What is the *modal verb* in each sentence?

1 We would like to discuss the problem.

2 I must leave at six o'clock.

3 I could find the station on the map.

4 I can jump over the fence.

5 We may buy some sweets.

6 I should get ready for school.

7 There might be some biscuits in the tin.

8 There might be snow this winter.

A Copy and complete the sentences with *can* or *may*.

1 This book is quite difficult but I am sure you _____ read it.

2 You _____ go out to play when you have changed your clothes.

3 He _____ get to the top of that tree without a ladder.

4 You _____ not cross the road by yourself.

B Copy and complete the sentences with *might* or *must*.

1 I _____ get some sleep because I need to be up early tomorrow.

2 He _____ finish his book if he reads quickly.

3 She _____ have toast or porridge for breakfast.

4 We _____ feed the cat before we go to school.

C Copy and complete the sentences with *could*, *would* or *should*.

1 I _____ write that letter in five minutes!

2 I _____ write the letter because he is waiting for a reply.

3 I _____ write that letter if my pen hadn't run out of ink.

Extension

Write sentences using these pairs of verbs.

Underline the *modal verb* in each sentence.

1 can sing

3 should tidy

5 would like

7 could find

9 can answer

2 must eat

4 may choose

6 might cook

8 must escape

10 may have

UNIT 25 Sentences

Sentences contain clauses.

A main clause is a sentence in itself.   The girl read the letter.

    It has a subject   = girl

    It has a predicate   = read the letter

    It has a proper verb in the predicate   = read

An adverb clause tells us more about the verb in the main clause.

An adverb clause begins with a conjunction.

    The girl read the letter before she went to school.

    main clause   = The girl read the letter

    adverb clause   = before she went to school

A relative clause tells us more about the noun in the main clause.

A relative clause begins with a relative pronoun.

 A relative clause is also known as an adjective clause.

    The girl read the letter that came from Australia.

    main clause   =   The girl read the letter

    relative clause   =   that came from Australia

Focus

Copy the sentences.

Underline the *main clauses*.

1 I want to see the man who won the race.
2 The man won the race because he ran so quickly.
3 You must have something to eat before you go out.
4 The winners were presented with the cup after the match had ended.
5 I will write neatly when I get a new pen.
6 This is the ball that broke the window.

Copy the sentences.

Underline any *adverb clauses* in red and *relative clauses* in blue.

1 Although it is a warm day, you must take your coats.

2 I have to wash the football shirts that are muddy.

3 The trip was cancelled because it had rained all night.

4 We will invite the twins who live on the farm.

5 Look at that duck whose beak is black!

6 He was nervous about the test even though he had worked hard.

Extension

A Copy and complete each sentence by adding a *relative clause*.

> Remember! Relative clauses begin with *who*, *whose*, *which*, *that*, *where* and *when*.

   1 This is the kitten _____

   2 Have you seen the rocket _____

   3 We saw the rider _____

   4 Can I speak to the teacher _____

B Copy and complete each sentence by adding an *adverb clause*.

   1 The little boy was naughty _____

   2 _____ will you let me know?

   3 The zebra walked to the waterhole _____

   4 You cannot watch that television programme _____

> Remember! Adverb clauses begin with a conjunction.

Commas are very useful for making what you write clear.
Using commas wrongly, or missing them out altogether, can make
it very difficult for a reader to know exactly what you mean!

1 The writer is telling Ella (her friend) that the
   cat is in the washing machine.
   Which sentence is correct?
   What does the other one mean?

   Ella the cat is in the washing machine!
   Ella, the cat is in the washing machine!

2 The writer is asking her mum if they can eat.
   Which sentence is correct?
   What does the other one mean?

   May we eat Mum?
   May we eat, Mum?

3 The writer is saying that Harry thinks Ben is confused.
   Which sentence is correct?
   What does the other one mean?

   Ben, thinks Harry, is confused.
   Ben thinks Harry is confused.

4 The writer is pleased that the soldier wasn't killed.
   Which sentence is correct?
   What does the other one mean?

   The soldier wasn't killed mercifully.
   The soldier wasn't killed, mercifully.

> **Ambiguity** is when
> a sentence could
> mean two very
> different things.

Focus

Explain what each sentence:

a means   **b** would mean without the *commas*.

1 Tony, my brother is happy.   **2** They applauded, thankfully.

3 The dog barked, strangely.   **4** Pat, thought Amy, was acting oddly.

5 May I paint, Dad?

Copy each sentence and add a *comma* or *commas* to change the meaning.

1 All the children sang happily.

2 Sophie the dog is eating my shoe!

3 Don't stop!

4 Harry imagined George was cheating.

5 May we shower Gran?

Explain the *difference* between each pair of sentences.

1 a I have just eaten my first pizza in a restaurant.

   b I have just eaten my first pizza, in a restaurant.

2 a The man with the walking stick pointed the way.

   b The man, with the walking stick, pointed the way.

3 a Most of the time, travellers are on edge.

   b Most of the time travellers are on edge.

4 a We give quality service and attention to detail.

   b We give quality, service and attention to detail.

5 a Slow children crossing.

   b Slow, children crossing.

6 a I love cooking my horse and my dog.

   b I love cooking, my horse and my dog.

Sometimes we want to put extra information in a sentence. When the extra information can be taken away and the sentence still makes sense, we can use any of these punctuation marks:

- commas

  Mrs Moira Green, who lives in Australia, has retired from the library after 60 years.

  sentence: Mrs Moira Green has retired from the library after 60 years.

  extra information: who lives in Australia

- brackets

  Midnight Star (a Grand National winner) is the favourite for today's big race.

  sentence: Midnight Star is the favourite for today's big race.

  extra information: a Grand National winner

- dashes

  The new supermarket – built against the wishes of the local people – will open on Saturday.

  sentence: The new supermarket will open on Saturday.

  extra information: built against the wishes of the local people

In each case, we can take out the words that come between the commas, brackets and dashes. We call this kind of extra information parenthesis.

Focus

Say what *extra information* has been added to each sentence.

1 A group of people, none of whom I knew, came into the shop.

2 The diagram (shown on page 25) illustrates the phases of the Moon.

3 The Dutch football team – minus some of their star players – were very impressive.

4 The first Moon landing, which took place in 1969, was watched by millions of people.

5 Buckingham Palace, now open to the public, is a famous London landmark.

Copy each sentence.

Choose *commas*, *brackets* or *dashes* to separate the extra information from the main sentence.

1 Aruba an island in the Caribbean Sea is a popular holiday destination.

2 All of the family except Aunt Susan came for my birthday.

3 The old bridge built in the 19th century badly needed repair.

4 The Chronicles of Narnia written by C S Lewis is a wonderful collection of novels.

5 Fill in the form use block capitals and black ink and return it in the prepaid envelope.

Extension

Make each pair of sentences into one sentence using *commas*, *brackets* or *dashes*.

> The first one has been done for you.

1 *Lake Garda is a beautiful place to visit.*

  It is situated in the north of Italy.

  Lake Garda, situated in the north of Italy, is a beautiful place to visit.

2 King penguins are amazing creatures.

  They are found in Antarctica.

3 Richard I lived in the 12th century.

  He was known as The Lionheart.

4 The Great Fire of London took place in 1666.

  It is generally believed to have started in Pudding Lane.

5 The Lord of the Rings is about the fight between good and evil.

  It was written by J R R Tolkien.

We need to look very carefully at what we write to see if we can improve it.

We can improve our writing by changing some of the vocabulary.

I had a nice time at the theme park.

wonderful   fantastic   amazing   exciting

"Look out!' she said.

shouted   yelled   cried   sobbed

We can improve our writing by expanding our sentences.

The elephant drank the water from the pool.

The large, grey elephant stretched out its long, flexible trunk to take a drink of refreshing water from the cool, shaded pool.

Look at each sentence you write and ask yourself if you could add more details to answer these questions:

What kind?
How many?   – adjectives / adjective phrases / relative clauses
How much?

When?
How?   – adverbs / adverb phrases / adverb clauses
Where?
How often?

Focus

Rewrite these sentences to *improve* them.

Replace the coloured words with more interesting ones.

1 Our nice hedge has grown a bit this spring.

2 "I've got a lot of work to do," said Harry.

3 I like cold weather because I've got a really warm coat.

4 "This book is good ," said Nancy.

Rewrite these sentences to give *details* that answer the questions in brackets.

1   The trees are growing.   (What kind? Where?)
2   The children played football.   (What kind? Where? How?)
3   The jockey won the race.   (What kind? When? How?)
4   Can you see the butterfly?   (What kind? Where?)
5   I walked into the valley.   (How? What kind? Where?)

Extension

Look carefully at each of the sentences below.

Rewrite them to include:

• more *interesting vocabulary*, replacing the words *got*, *said*, *like*, *nice*, *lot*, *big* and *little*.

• *words*, *phrases* and *clauses* that give the reader more *detail*.

1   A little bird sat on a tree.

2   The bus got stuck.

3   "I've lost my ticket," said Sita.

4   I would like an ice cream.

5   The wind was a bit strong.

6   I got a nice jacket.

7   You can get a lot in the bucket.

8   "Did you have a nice time?" said Dad.

9   "Did you see the big bull?" said Katy.

10 That meal was nice.

How to use this book

The heading tells you what the grammar topic is.

The information box tells you about the grammar topic.

The owl gives you extra information.

UNIT
3 **Verbs**

 This is a round-up of the verb tenses you know.

Verbs tell us what happens, has happened or will happen.

The tense of a verb tells us when something happens – in the past, the present or the future.

- past simple tense — He found a beautiful island.
- past progressive tense — He was travelling by boat.
- perfect tense — He has been around the world.
- past perfect tense — He had explored before.
- present simple tense — He likes exploring.
- present progressive tense — He is enjoying the trip.
- future tense — He will go to sea again.

Focus

A Say the verb tenses with I for each verb.

| past simple | past progressive | perfect | past perfect |
| present simple | present progressive | future | |

1 to climb 2 to eat 3 to speak 4 to draw 5 to think 6 to swim

B Identify the verb in each sentence and say which tense it is.

1 The cat was walking on the narrow wall.
2 The ladder fell with a crash.
3 He had forgotten his car keys.
4 We shall visit at the weekend.
5 I have seen that film before.

10

Practice

A Write these sentences in the present progressive tense and the past progressive tense.

1 I go for a walk.
2 They ride their horses.
3 We swim.

B Write these sentences in the perfect tense and the past perfect tense.

1 The birds flew away.
2 My strap broke.
3 They ate.

C Write these sentences in the present simple tense and the past simple tense.

1 I shall leave.
2 The sun will set.
3 You will go.

Extension

Write a sentence in the past tense and the future tense that includes each pair of actions.

Action 1: happens first
Action 2: happens second

The first one has been done for you.

Action 1	Action 2
1 go to the park	go again tomorrow
I went to the park and I shall go again tomorrow.	
2 finish loaf of bread	buy more
3 dig garden	plant seeds
4 wash clothes	iron clothes

11

You might want to discuss these questions with a talk partner before answering them.

The tips box tells you more about answering the question.

Sometimes your teacher might ask you to fill in Activity Sheets.

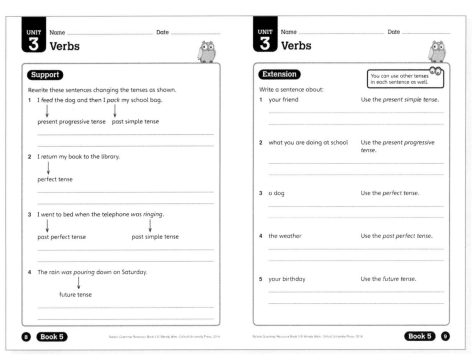

UNIT **3** Name _____ Date _____

Verbs

Support

Rewrite these sentences changing the tenses as shown.

1 I *feed* the dog and then I *pack* my school bag.
   ↓ present progressive tense   ↓ past simple tense
   _____

2 I *return* my book to the library.
   ↓ perfect tense
   _____

3 I *went* to bed when the telephone *was ringing*.
   ↓ past perfect tense   ↓ past simple tense
   _____

4 The rain *was pouring* down on Saturday.
   ↓ future tense
   _____

8 **Book 5**

Nelson Grammar Resource Book 3 © Wendy Wren, Oxford University Press, 2014

UNIT **3** Name _____ Date _____

Verbs

Extension

> You can use other tenses in each sentence as well.

Write a sentence about:

1 your friend   Use the *present simple tense.*
   _____

2 what you are doing at school   Use the *present progressive tense.*
   _____

3 a dog   Use the *perfect tense.*
   _____

4 the weather   Use the *past perfect tense.*
   _____

5 your birthday   Use the *future tense.*
   _____

Nelson Grammar Resource Book 3 © Wendy Wren, Oxford University Press, 2014

Book 5 9

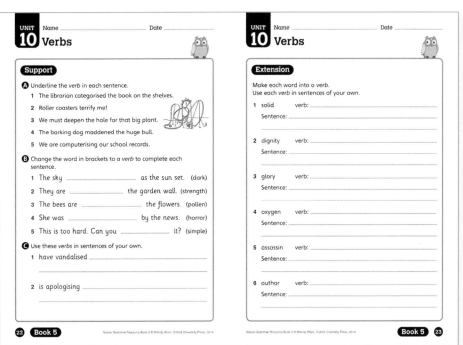

UNIT **10** Name _____ Date _____

Verbs

Support

A Underline the *verb* in each sentence.
   1 The librarian categorised the book on the shelves.
   2 Roller coasters terrify me!
   3 We must deepen the hole for that big plant.
   4 The barking dog maddened the huge bull.
   5 We are computerising our school records.

B Change the word in brackets to a *verb* to complete each sentence.
   1 The sky _____ as the sun set.   (dark)
   2 They are _____ the garden wall. (strength)
   3 The bees are _____ the flowers. (pollen)
   4 She was _____ by the news.   (horror)
   5 This is too hard. Can you _____ it? (simple)

C Use these *verbs* in sentences of your own.
   1 have vandalised _____
   2 is apologising _____

22 **Book 5**

Nelson Grammar Resource Book 3 © Wendy Wren, Oxford University Press, 2014

UNIT **10** Name _____ Date _____

Verbs

Extension

Make each word into a *verb.*
Use each *verb* in sentences of your own.

1 solid   verb: _____
   Sentence: _____

2 dignity   verb: _____
   Sentence: _____

3 glory   verb: _____
   Sentence: _____

4 oxygen   verb: _____
   Sentence: _____

5 assassin   verb: _____
   Sentence: _____

6 author   verb: _____
   Sentence: _____

Nelson Grammar Resource Book 3 © Wendy Wren, Oxford University Press, 2014

Book 5 23